To
Debbie
Family, Friends
& Food
Love
Happy - Don't Thank

Eric Neri 7/07

Eric Neri
Executive Chef

Ice Cream to Caviar

DON CESAR BEACH RESORT
A LOEWS HOTEL
ST PETE BEACH

ESPICHEL ENTERPRISES, PUBLISHERS

The Don CeSar Hotel was the lifelong dream of Florida real estate tycoon Thomas Rowe, but by the time it opened in 1928, its $1.2 million price tag was nearly 300 percent over budget and had exhausted all of Rowe's capital. However, he knew he had created something special and the world, even to this day, knew it as well. In those early days it was the place to be and the place to be seen, and people from all facets of high society flocked to The Don.

Thomas Rowe

FLORIDA AUTO TRAILS TO

DON CE-SAR
HOTEL

THE KINGDOM OF THE SUN

1928

The design of The Don was a combination of Mediterranean and Moorish influences with stucco and tile walls, red clay tile roofs, arched openings and towers on the upper stories. Over the front entrance Thomas Rowe had a hotel greeting carved : "Come all ye who seek health and rest for here they are abundant". A frequent guest, F. Scott Fitzgerald referred to it as "a hotel in an island wilderness" in many of his books.

Originally designed as a 225 room hotel, Rowe enlarged it to include 325 rooms with private baths and 100 bathing rooms for changing on the beach. He also added 100 rooms for his hotel staff and a garage for parking 100 automobiles.

On January 16, 1928, three years late and 300% over budget, The Don was ready for guests. More than fifteen hundred arrived for the premier opening to celebrate the evening in the grand ballroom on the fifth floor with exquisite dining and dancing, all for the modest fee of $2.50.

In its hey day, The Don attracted some of the most influential and wealthy families in the world. Babe Ruth and Lou Gehrig, Al Capone and Clarence Darrow, F. Scott Fitzgerald, Mariel Hemmingway and President Franklin D. Roosevelt were among the celebrated guests.

1930-73

Then came three major catastrophes, the Depression, World War II and the death of Thomas Rowe. His final wish to will his masterpiece to his employees was never signed and sole ownership went to his estranged wife of 30 years. In less than three years, the charm and personality of The Don was all but lost and she sold The Pink Palace to the U.S. Army as a convalescent center. After the war it was stripped for use as offices of the Veterans Administration until 1967 when they moved, unable to afford the necessary repairs.

Abandoned and forgotten by everyone except graffiti artists, The Pink Lady seemed destined for the wrecking ball until a persistent and diligent preservation group found a buyer who shared Thomas Rowe's vision of grandeur and elegance. In 1973, after extensive renovations, The Don CeSar reopened its doors as a luxury beach resort.

ZELDA'S
SEASIDE CAFE

From its opening, the first menus assured guests that the cuisine at The Don was going to be as elegant as the architectural ambiance and service of the Pink Palace.

It was the age of the flapper, and The Don was "the place to be" for dining and dancing by the seashore. Zelda's was one of the first cafes on Florida's west coast to offer superb cuisine in a casual setting overlooking the Gulf of Mexico.

The King Charles Room opened a new era of elegant dining at The Don where guests were served on linens with silver and stemware under crystal chandeliers as a harp was played in the background.

Mr. Thomas Rowe was a teetotaler, but following prohibition he allowed a new bar and lounge to be opened in the upper lobby of The Don.

The original Maritana Grille was opened in 1993 on the lobby level as the premier dining room of the Don. Here guests could enjoy five course dinners with a choice of fine wines in the most elaborate setting of the times.

The Don CeSar Beach Resort, A Loews Hotel, is once again the crown jewel of Florida's Gulf Coast beaches. Several multi-million dollar renovations have rejuvenated a feeling of refined luxury and superior service that has been a hallmark of "The Pink Palace" since 1928.

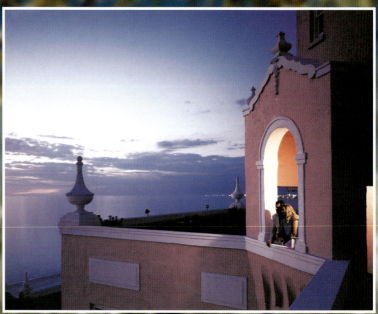

Guests of The Don enjoy a world of amenities and activities. From a rejuvenated lobby with a rich mahogany bar, to enhanced guest rooms, the feeling of pampering and indulgence reigns supreme. An avant-garde European style spa offers an array of massage and treatments, personal trainers and exercise instructors to stimulate and renew each guest.

The Pink Palace sports two heated outdoor swimming pools, a heated jacuzzi and a sugar-white sand beach ideal for sunbathing or a sunset stroll. Golf and tennis are nearby as well as scuba diving, sailing and fishing just offshore. It also boasts some 40,000 square feet of multi-functional spaces for business meetings and private parties.

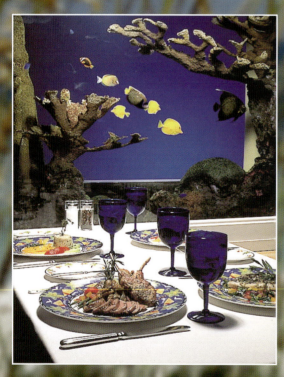

Dining at the Don is a culinary treat to please every taste, from 38 flavors at Uncle Andy's Ice Cream Parlor, to caviar at The Maritana Grille. Our signature Four Diamond restaurant features creative New American Cuisine from salmon to souffle, prepared over a pecan and cherry wood grill. For a truly unique dining experience, The Chef's Table, nestled in a corner of the Maritana kitchen, serves one-of-a-kind creations for private parties of eight.

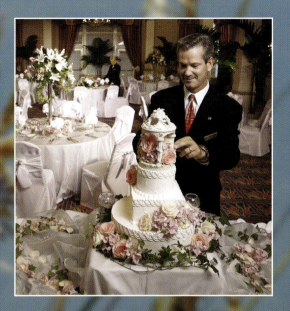

This majestic wedding setting rises from the sugary Gulf shores of St. Pete Beach, with its flamingo pink walls and lush tropical gardens sharply contrasting against the blue Florida sky. The Don CeSar Beach Resort, A Loews Hotel, affectionately known as The Pink Palace, has hosted thousands of dream weddings.

The Culinary Staff of The Don CeSar Beach Resort, directed by Executive Chef Eric Neri, is an award winning team of professionals who cater to guests' every taste, from casual poolside fare to haute cuisine at their Four Diamond Maritana Grille. The recipes which follow are favorite selections of Chef Neri's world class gourmet creations he designs for dining at The Don.

Caviar & Semolina Crostini

4 oz Beluga caviar
1 semolina baguette
1/2 cup butter
1/2 cup minced shallots
!/2 cup minced chives
1/2 cup creme fraiche
1/2 cup minced egg whites
1/2 cup minced egg yolks

For the Semolina Crostini:
Thinly slice the semolina baguette. Spread a light coat of butter on both sides of each slice. Grill them until they are toasted on both sides. Place some minced shallots on each slice.

Place the caviar in mother of pearl spoons and display around the egg whites, yolks, chives and creme fraiche. Serve with crostinis.

Tuna Tartare with Sweet Sushi Rice

1 cup finely diced tuna
1/4 cup minced green onions
1/2 cup sweet chili sauce
1/2 cup sushi rice (pg 105)
1 cup shiitake mushroom puree
flat parsley for garnish

For Shiitake Mushroom Puree:
3 cups julienned shiitake mushrooms
1/4 cup oyster sauce
1/4 cup sweet soy sauce
4 tblsps brown sugar
1 tblsp bonito flakes
1/4 cup soy sauce
1/4 cup water
1 tblsp chiffonade cilantro
1 tblsp julienned pickled ginger
salt & pepper to taste

For shiitake mushroom puree: Combine all ingredients in a heavy saucepan. Cook over medium heat until all liquids have been absorbed and mushrooms are glazed. Puree and chill.

Toss the diced tuna and green onions together. Add the sweet chili sauce to the tuna mixture and let set for 2 to 3 minutes. Note: the glaze has all the spices to season the tuna. Serve the tuna in Asian style spoons with shiitake mushroom puree over a small amount of sushi rice. Garnish spoons with parsley leaves.

Tuna Nicoise Hors D'Oeuvre on Risotto Cakes

For the Tuna:

1/2 lb Ahi tuna, diced small
1/4 cup minced french green beans
2 tblsps minced capers
2 tblsps minced calamata olives

1 tblsp minced red onion
2 tblsps minced tomato
1 tblsp minced green onion
2 tblsps olive oil
salt & pepper to taste

Mix all ingredients and season with salt and pepper, then chill. Using two teaspoons, quenelle the tuna and serve on risotto cakes.

For the Risotto Cakes:
2 cups flour
4 eggs, beaten

salt & pepper to taste
2 cups panko bread crumbs
2 cups olive oil

Remove risotto from freezer and cut into rounds using a small cutter. Season the flour with salt and pepper. Dredge all rounds in flour, egg and panko bread crumbs. Heat the olive oil to medium and brown each risotto cake on both sides. Drain on paper towels, cool to room temperature and top with tuna nicoise.

For the Risotto:
1 cup arborio rice
2-1/2 cups chicken stock
4 tblsps olive oil
1/4 cup diced onion
1/2 cup diced shiitake mushrooms
1 medium pepper, diced
2 tblsps chiffonade basil
1 tsp minced fresh thyme
1/4 cup shredded asiago
salt & pepper to taste

Saute the onion, mushrooms and pepper in the oil until soft. Add the rice and mix until it is coated with the oil. Add enough stock to cover the rice and continue to stir until the liquid is absorbed. Keep adding more stock a little at a time while stirring until all the liquid is absorbed and the rice is tender. Then season with basil, thyme, asiago cheese, salt and pepper. Spread the risotto evenly on a sheet tray about 1/4" thick and freeze until firm.

Bacon Wrapped Lobster,
Lump Crab Salad
& Citrus Vinaigrette

4 Maine lobster tails, 6 oz each
32 slices slab bacon (butcher sliced)
1 lb lump crab meat
1/2 cup diced red tomato

1 tblsp minced chives
1/2 cup diced mango
1/2 cup citrus vinaigrette (pg 96)
salt & pepper to taste

Skewer the lobster tails to keep them straight while cooking. Place the tails in a large pot of boiling water for 4 minutes. Remove and place them in an ice bath. When cool, carefully remove the tail meat whole from the shells. Lay out bacon slices slightly overlapping, eight slices per tail. Place the lobster tails on the bacon, bottom side up. Roll the bacon so the seams meet on the bottom of the tails. Sear the tails on medium heat, bottom side first. Once seared, roll the tails and sear the other side until golden brown. Place the tails, seam side down, in a 350° oven for about 5 minutes, checking to see they do not over cook. Remove and set aside.

For the Crab Salad: Toss the chilled crab meat, chives, mango and tomatoes with the citrus vinaigrette. Season with salt and pepper.

Slice the warm lobster tails and serve with the chilled lump crab salad.

Jumbo Lump Crab, Sweet & Sour Mango Napoleon

Serves four

8 oz jumbo lump crab meat
1 cup diced fresh mango
1/4 cup diced red pepper
1/4 cup chiffonade green onion
2 tblsps chiffonade basil
2 tblsps fresh lime juice
2 tblsps sweet chili sauce
1/2 cup micro greens
salt & pepper to taste

Combine crab meat, peppers, basil and green onions. Mix in lime juice and sweet chili sauce. Season and set aside. Using a 4" ring mold to assemble, pack with crab mixture 2/3 full, then finish last 1/3 with diced mango. Unmold and top with micro greens. Garnish plates with sweet chili sauce.

For the Terrine:
11 oz goat cheese
1/2 cup chiffonade basil
2 tblsps roasted garlic puree

1-1/2 cups clarified butter
3 large Idaho potatoes, peeled
2 egg yolks
salt & pepper to taste

Slice the potatoes 1/16" thick, lengthwise, and place them in a bowl of warm water. Remove from water, place on parchment lined sheet tray and brush with clarified butter. Cover with another parchment sheet and place in a 250° oven for 6 to 8 minutes. Remove and let cool. Combine the goat cheese, basil, roasted garlic in a bowl, season with salt and pepper and chill. Line a 2"x1"x12" terrine mold with plastic wrap and cover bottom with overlapping potato slices. Fill terrine 1/2 way evenly with goat cheese mixture. Top with 2 layers of potato slices and fill terrine with remaining goat cheese. Cover with overlapping potato slices and seal with plastic wrap. Wrap terrine with foil and bake in a 250° oven for 30 minutes. Place weight on top and refrigerate overnight.

Remove, unmold and cut into 1/2 inch slices. Sear the terrine slices on both sides in butter on high heat. Arrange beet slices on plate. Season greens with salt and pepper, toss in truffle vinaigrette and place over beets. Lean slices of the terrine over the greens and garnish plate with red pepper juice and basil oil.

Serves four

8 potato terrine slices
2 tblsps clarified butter
4 oz micro greens
1 cup truffle vinaigrette (pg 96)
12 roasted beet slices
2 tblsps red pepper juice (pg 98)
1 tblsp basil oil

Potato & Herbed
Goat Cheese Terrine

Ahi Tuna & Lump Crab Timbale with Soy Vinaigrette

Serves four

1/2 lb Ahi tuna, diced
1/2 lb jumbo lump crab meat
1/2 tblsp diced red pepper
1/2 tblsp diced yellow pepper
1 tblsp diced red tomato
1 tblsp diced yellow tomato
1 tblsp chiffonade chives
2 tsps rice wine vinegar
1 tsp sesame oil
salt and pepper to taste
8 orange sections
1/2 cup micro sprouts
1/2 cup soy vinaigrette (pg 97)

Combine all ingredients except orange sections, micro sprouts and vinaigrette. Mix well and chill for ten minutes. Fill 3 inch ring molds 3/4 full. To serve, unmold and garnish with micro sprouts. Arrange orange sections and drizzle plates with soy vinaigrette.

Ahi Tuna with Sweet Asian Glaze & Pickled Ginger Salad

Serves four

1/2 lb Ahi tuna loin
1 tblsp allspice
1 tblsp curry powder
1 tblsp paprika
1 tblsp ginger powder
1 tblsp black pepper

1 tblsp sesame oil
2 tblsps olive oil
1/2 cup sweet Asian glaze (pg 103)
1 tblsp wasabi
1 tblsp sesame seeds
shrimp chips
4 tblsps pickled ginger salad

Blend all of the spices together and pat onto tuna loin. Heat oils and sear the tuna on all sides until just rare, then cool. Wrap in plastic wrap and chill for 1 hour. Slice into very thin medallions, leaving the plastic wrap on to hold the meat together. After removing the wrap, serve with pickled ginger salad, Asian glaze, shrimp chips and wasabi rolled in sesame seeds.

Balsamic Glazed Salmon, Steak & Lump Crab Salad

Serves four

4 salmon steaks, 12 oz each
1-1/2 cups balsamic vinegar
2 tblsps olive oil
salt and pepper to taste
12 each red and yellow grape tomatoes

Make a glaze by reducing the vinegar to
1/2 cup and cool. Coat the salmon with
half of the glaze. Pan sear the steaks in
olive oil over medium heat on both sides until
golden brown, but not fully cooked. Bake
the steaks at 350° for 4 to 5 minutes, keeping
the fish moist inside (thicker steaks may
take a few more minutes). Drizzle salmon
with some glaze and top with the crab
salad. Toss tomatoes with remaining
glaze and place around the salmon.

Lump Crab Salad
1/2 lb lump crab meat
1 cup frisée greens
1 cup watercress
1/2 cup julienned watermelon radish
2 shallots, julienned
1/4 cup Petite Syrah vinaigrette (pg 97)
salt and pepper to taste

Toss all salad ingredients
together with the
vinaigrette, then season
with salt and pepper.

Pan Seared Diver Scallops,
Lobster Risotto & Persicus Caviar

Serves four
16 large diver scallops
1 tblsp olive oil
1 large red beet
salt and pepper to taste
1-1/2 tblsps Persicus caviar
1/2 cup citrus vinaigrette
       (pg 96)

Salt and pepper the beet after brushing with olive oil and roast in a 350° oven for 1 hour. Remove, cool then chill for two hours. Skin and slice the beet thinly and cut into 16 circles using a 1" cutter. Season circles and lightly saute in butter. Salt and pepper the scallops then pan sear in olive oil over high heat until golden brown. Finish in a 350° oven for 3 minutes until medium inside. Drain well on paper towels. Place each scallop on a beet slice and top with caviar. Arrange around the risotto topped with micro sprouts, drizzle with citrus vinaigrette and garnish with orange segments.

Lobster Risotto
2-1/2 cups arborio rice
1 cup cooked lobster meat
6 cups lobster stock
5 tblsps olive oil
1 medium onion, chopped
1/4 cup white wine

Cook the onions in olive oil over medium heat until tender. Add rice and stir to coat with oil. Add wine and cook until evaporated, stirring constantly. Add 1/3 cup stock and cook until absorbed, stirring constantly. Repeat process until all stock is used and rice is tender. Remove from heat and add lobster.

35

Lobster Agnolotti
with Micro Sprouts

Serves four

Filling

8 oz lobster meat, uncooked
1 tblsp julienned leeks
4 tblsps julienned shiitake mushrooms
1/2 tblsp chopped roasted garlic
1/2 tblsp julienned fresh basil
1/3 cup heavy cream
1 oz asiago cheese, grated
1 tsp white truffle oil
salt and pepper to taste

Sauté leeks and mushrooms then chill. In a food processor, combine lobster, mushrooms and leeks, garlic and basil. Puree quickly then slowly add cream. Continue to puree until smooth then pour into a bowl. Fold in cheese, truffle oil and season to taste. Refrigerate.

Pasta

4 cups all purpose flour
5 extra large eggs
1 tblsp olive oil
1 tblsp salt

Using a fork, create a well in the flour and place eggs, olive oil and salt in the center. Slowly incorporate flour until dough forms a ball. Continue until all flour is incorporated, then refrigerate. Starting with #1 setting, roll dough through a pasta machine several times, ending with #6 setting. Place 1 tablespoon of the lobster filling on half of the rolled pasta sheet 1-1/2 inches apart. Fold the sheet over and cut into agnolotti shapes. Place in boiling water and cook for 3 minutes. Drain well.

1/2 cup diced & seeded tomatoes
1 tblsp minced shallots
1 tblsp butter
1 cup lobster beurre blanc (pg 103)
4 tblsps micro sprouts

Lightly heat the tomatoes and shallots in butter until soft. Remove from heat and toss with agnolotti. Place beurre blanc in a bowl, add agnolottis and top with micro sprouts.

Princess Paella with
Saffron Risotto

Serves four

4 mahi fillets, 3 oz each
salt & pepper to taste
12 butter clams
12 mussels
8 medium Gulf shrimp
1 lb chorizo sausage, sliced
1 cup diced tomatoes
1 tblsp chiffonade cilantro
1 cup diced white onion
1/2 cup white wine
3/4 cup olive oil
8 oz whole butter
25 roasted tomato slices (pg 98)
1-1/2 cups fish stock (pg 99)
1 lb saffron risotto (pg 104)

Place half the olive oil in a
shallow pot and cook onions
until wilted. Add the wine
and clams and cook for two
minutes. Add fish stock,
bring to a boil, whisk in butter
and lower heat. Add shrimp,
sausage, mussels, diced and
roasted tomatoes, then season with
cilantro, salt and pepper. Cook for
two minutes more and remove from heat.
Season mahi fillets with salt and pepper
and pan sear one to two minutes on each
side. Place the saffron risotto in the paella pan.
Arrange the seafood and sausage around the
rice and bake in a 350°oven for ten to fifteen
minutes. Drizzle with remaining olive oil.

Horseradish Crusted Salmon with Shrimp & Vegetable Fricassee

Serves four

4 salmon fillets, 7 oz each
1/4 cup horseradish
1/2 cup dijon mustard
3/4 cup julienned vegetables
8 oz baby shrimp
1-1/2 cups lobster beurre blanc (pg 103)
1/4 cup raspberry sauce
3/4 cup panko bread crumbs
3 oz butter
salt & pepper to taste

Combine the horseradish and mustard and coat salmon fillets with the mixture, then coat with panko bread crumbs. Sear fillets in oil, then finish cooking in a 325° oven. Sauté vegetables in butter, then add shrimp and the lobster beurre blanc. Center the vegetables on plates, arrange shrimp around and place fillet on top. Add remaining sauce to plate and garnish with raspberry sauce and edible orchid.

Root Vegetable Shrimp Salad

6 large shrimp, shelled & deveined
16 broccoli raab stalks
6 baby red carrots
8 round orange carrots
3 baby yellow beets
1/2 red onion, julienned
2 watermelon radishes
1/4 cup olive oil
juice of 2 large lemons
1 tblsp rice wine vinegar
2 tblsps minced shallots
1 tblsp minced fresh tarragon
kosher salt & black pepper to taste

Blanch the carrots, beets and broccoli raab separately in boiling salted water until crisp but not raw. Refrigerate to chill.

Steep a herb sash of tarragon, lemon grass, white and red peppercorns in simmering water for 5 minutes, then bring to a boil. Add shrimp to boiling water for 4–6 minutes. Remove shrimp and chill. Toss all vegetables and shrimp with the lemon juice, olive oil, vinegar, tarragon, shallots and season with salt and pepper before serving.

Ahi Tuna & Avocado Roll with Asian Slaw

Serves four

1/2 lb Ahi tuna
1 avocado
4 scallions, julienned

1/2 red pepper, julienned
2 tblsps pickled ginger
1/2 cup wasabi mayonnaise (pg 101)
2 chili tortilla wraps (12 inch)

Spread the wasabi mayonnaise on the tortilla wraps. Cut the tuna into thin strips. Peel and pit the avocado and slice thin. Place the tuna, avocado, ginger, pepper and scallions in the tortilla wraps, roll up tight and set aside.

For the Asian Slaw:
1 cup shredded Napa cabbage
1/4 cup julienned red onion
1/4 cup julienned red & yellow pepper

2 tblsps chopped cilantro
1/2 cup pickled ginger salad
1/4 cup soy vinaigrette (pg 97)
lotus root as garnish

Place all the vegetables in a bowl, add the vinaigrette and toss. Add more vinaigrette if desired. Slice the tuna rolls and serve with Asian Slaw. Garnish with lotus root chips.

Pan Seared Sea Scallops, Vanilla Bean Mashed Potatoes and Beluga Caviar

Serves four

8 large sea scallops
1/4 cup each Parisienne carrots, zucchini, yellow squash
1 tblsp minced shallot
1/4 cup white wine
3/4 cup fish stock (pg 99)
6 oz whole butter
1 tblsp chiffonade opal basil
salt & pepper to taste
vanilla bean mashed potatoes (pg 99)
4 gaufrette potatoes
2 oz Beluga caviar
4 sprigs opal basil

Lightly saute the shallots in 2 oz of butter until wilted. Add the wine and cook for about 2 minutes. Add the Parisienne vegetables and fish stock and bring to a boil. After two minutes add the rest of the butter and whisk to emulsify the stock. Add the chiffonade basil, season with salt and pepper and set aside.

Season the scallops with salt and pepper and sear over high heat on both sides. Lower the heat and finish for 2 to 3 minutes or until scallops are medium inside. Reheat the vegetables in the broth. Spoon the mashed potatoes into serving bowls and add the vegetables and broth. Add the scallops, top each with Beluga caviar and garnish with gaufrette potato and basil sprig.

Dover Sole,
Baby Spinach & Tomato Confit

48

Season the Dover sole with salt and pepper, then lightly dredge in flour. Shake off excess flour and set aside. Heat a large teflon saute pan and add the clarified butter. When hot, add the sole and cook 2 to 3 minutes or until golden brown on each side. Place in a casserole dish, add 4 oz butter, 3/4 cup wine and bake at 350° for 8 to 10 minutes.

Carefully remove the fillets from the center bone. Cut the center bone in half and coat the tips in paprika for garnish. Place the fillets back together around the bone. Cook shallots in remaining whole butter over medium heat until soft. Increase heat, add remaining 1/4 cup wine and reduce by half. Add spinach and season with salt and pepper. Place spinach on plate, add tomato confit and place sole on top.

Serves four

4 each 1-1/4 lbs Dover sole, skinned
3 cups flour
salt & pepper
1/4 cup clarified butter
5 oz whole butter
1 cup white wine
2 tblsps minced shallots
6 oz baby spinach
2 cups tomato confit (pg 98)

Wood Grilled Prosciutto Wrapped Prawns

Serves four

12 large prawns
12 thin prosciutto slices
1 small vidalia onion
3/4 cup fish stock (pg 99)
1/4 cup heavy cream
1 roasted garlic head
2 roasted plum tomatoes
1/2 cup julienned yellow tomato
2 tblsps chiffonade basil
2 tblsps butter
1/2 lb fettuccine, cooked al dente
grated asiago cheese to taste
salt and pepper to taste

Slice the onion into thin rings and season with salt and pepper. Grill rings on both sides until golden brown. Once cooled, cut the rings in half and dice small. Reduce the fish stock by half, then add the cream and cook on medium heat for 2 minutes. Add the garlic, tomatoes, basil, onions and butter, then reduce the heat. Simmer for 2 to 3 minutes, stirring constantly, until sauce is slightly thickened.

Wrap each prawn with a slice of prosciutto and grill slowly for 3 minutes on each side being careful not to over cook. Pour the sauce over the cooked pasta centered in plates. Arrange the prawns around the pasta and garnish with asiago cheese.

Crispy Yellowtail Snapper, Tomato & Olive Ragout

Serves four

4 snapper fillets, 6 oz each
3/4 cup fish stock (pg 99)
1/4 cup sliced calamata olives
1-1/2 tblsps roasted garlic puree
1/4 cup diced tomatoes
1/4 cup julienned spinach
3 oz butter
salt & pepper to taste
1/3 cup diced yukon gold potatoes, cooked
2 tblsps chopped scallions
4 tblsps sliced salsify, cooked
1 tblsp olive oil
2 cups julienned carrots,
    zucchini & yellow squash
flour
oil for frying

Combine fish stock and butter and bring to a boil while stirring. Reduce heat to low, add all vegetables and continue to stir until just done. Meanwhile season fish and sear on both sides in olive oil until just cooked through. Spoon vegetables onto plate and place fish on top. Season carrots and squash, lightly dust with flour and deep fry in oil. Add remaining sauce to plate and top with fried vegetables.

Florida Cioppino

2 Florida lobster tails
8 oz red snapper fillets
4 large gulf shrimp
8 stone crab claws
2 tblsps minced shallots
1 tsp minced garlic
2 tblsps olive oil
2 cipollini onions
8 round carrots
1 lb pea vines
2 cups sliced red potatoes
1/2 cup diced red & yellow tomatoes
1 tsp chopped flat parsley
4 cups fish stock (pg 99)
1/2 cup white wine
salt & pepper to taste

In a large shallow pot on medium heat, cook the garlic and shallots in olive oil until soft. Add the white wine and reduce by half. Add the fish stock, potatoes, onions and cook about 2 minutes, then add the lobster tails in shells, carrots and cook another 5 minutes. Add the shrimp and simmer for 3 more minutes. Cut the snapper into four 2 oz pieces, season with salt and pepper and pan sear in olive oil on both sides for 2 minutes, then remove from heat. Finally add the snapper, stone crab claws and pea vines to the seafood pot. Season with salt and pepper. Display on a large platter and garnish with parsley and flat bread.

Pan Seared Halibut
in White Asparagus Celery Broth

Serves four

4 halibut fillets, 7 oz each

3 tblsps olive oil

1/2 lb white asparagus, sliced

1/2 lb celery, sliced

4 cups fish stock (pg 99)

1/4 cup white wine

1/2 lb red & yellow baby pear tomatoes, halved

4 oz butter

2 tblsps chopped chives

salt and pepper to taste

8 white asparagus spears for garnish

Season each fillet with salt and pepper. Heat the olive oil over medium heat and sear the halibut for 1 to 2 minutes on each side. Finish in a 350° oven for 6 to 8 minutes.

For White Asparagus Celery Broth: Add the celery to the fish stock and begin reducing over medium high heat. When the celery is half cooked, add the sliced asparagus and white wine. Once the celery and asparagus are tender, add the pear tomatoes. Season to taste, then add the butter and chives. Spoon broth into bowls, top each with a halibut fillet and garnish with 2 asparagus spears and celery leaf.

Serves four

4 mahi fillets, 6 oz each
12 large prawns
4 tblsps blackening spice
2 tblsps clarified butter
2 tblsps whole butter
1/4 cup white wine

2 roasted garlic cloves, minced
salt and pepper to taste
1/2 cup vanilla beurre blanc
1/2 cup papaya banana chutney
2 cups coconut jasmine rice

Sprinkle the tops of the fillets with blackening spice. Place mahi, seasoned side down first, in clarified butter over medium heat. Cook for 1 minute on each side. Finish in a 350° oven for 4 minutes, depending on the thickness of the fish, keeping it firm and moist. Season the prawns with salt and pepper, then grill for 2–3 minutes on each side. Heat garlic in butter, add the wine and reduce by half. Add prawns and heat until warm. Serve the fillets over rice (pg 105), top with the prawns and chutney (pg 100) then drizzle with vanilla buerre blanc (pg 103)

Blackened Mahi & Grilled Prawns
with Coconut Jasmine Rice

Crab & Scallop Galette
with Frisée Greens and
Truffle Vinaigrette

Serves four

6 scallops (v-10 dry pack)
6 oz jumbo lump crab meat
2 tblsps chopped shallots
2 tblsps chopped truffles
4 tblsps brandy
1/3 cup heavy cream
1 tblsp julienned basil
1-1/2 oz grated asiago cheese
1 tsp white truffle oil

egg wash
flour
bread crumbs
salt and pepper to taste
micro sprouts
16 orange segments
citrus vinaigrette (pg 96)

Combine shallots, truffles, brandy and simmer until dry, then chill. Puree scallops in a food processor and add cream until smooth. Combine scallop puree with crab meat, shallot mixture, basil, cheese, truffle oil and season to taste. Using plastic wrap, roll mixture into 6 to 8 inch logs, 1 inch in diameter. Steam for 10 minutes, then chill for two hours. Unwrap chilled galette, roll in seasoned flour, dip in egg wash, then coat with panko bread crumbs. Fry in hot oil until golden brown, then cut into 1/2 inch slices. Place salad in the center of plates and top with micro sprouts. Surround the salad with slices of galette and garnish with orange segments and citrus vinaigrette.

Frisée Greens
3 cups frisée greens
1/4 cup julienned red pepper
1/4 cup julienned red onion
1/4 cup julienned carrot
3 tblsps truffle vinaigrette (pg 96)

Toss all ingredients with truffle vinaigrette.
Season with salt and pepper.

Seabass, Lobster Salad
& Papaya Banana Ravioli

Serves four

4 seabass fillets, skin on, 7 oz each
2 tblsps olive oil
2 cups each, green & yellow pea shoots
6 oz cooked lobster meat, diced
2 shallots, chopped

2 tblsps sliced chives
3/4 cup citrus vinaigrette
24 orange segments
4 papaya ravioli (pg 100)
salt and pepper to taste

Heat the oil on medium heat. Season the fillets with salt and pepper then sear, skin side down first, 1 to 2 minutes on each side. Finish in a 350° oven for 5 to 7 minutes or until medium inside. Make a salad by combining the lobster meat, pea shoots, shallots, chives and half of the citrus vinaigrette (pg 96). Season with salt and pepper and toss well. Place the salad in the center of plates and top each with a fillet of seabass. Garnish with orange segments, ravioli and remaining citrus vinaigrette.

Lobster Cannelloni, Wilted Leeks & Shiitake Mushrooms

Serves four

Filling
1-1/2 cups lobster meat, uncooked
1/4 cup julienned shiitake mushrooms
2 tblsps julienned leeks
1 tblsp butter

3 roasted garlic cloves
2 tblsps julienned basil
1/3 cup heavy cream
1 tsp grated asiago cheese
1 tsp white truffle oil

Saute the mushrooms and leeks in butter until soft, then cool. In a food processor, puree the lobster meat, mushrooms and leeks, garlic and basil. Slowly add the cream until fully incorporated and smooth. Place in a bowl, fold in the cheese, truffle oil, season to taste then refrigerate.

Pasta
4 cups all purpose flour
5 extra large eggs
1 tblsp olive oil
pinch of salt

Garnish
4 lobster claws
1/2 cup julienned leeks
1/2 cup diced tomatoes
2 tblsps butter
1 cup lobster beurre blanc (pg 103)

For Pasta: Using a fork, create a well in the flour and place eggs, oil and salt in the center. Slowly incorporate flour with eggs and oil until dough forms a ball. Continue until all flour is incorporated, then refrigerate. Starting with the #1 setting, roll pasta dough through a pasta machine several times, ending with the #6 setting. Cut the pasta into 4 inch square sheets. Blanch the sheets in boiling water for 30 seconds. Shock in cold water and pat dry. On each sheet, place 2 to 3 oz of filling in the middle and roll into cannelloni shapes. Cut each end of the cannelloni on the bias. Steam for 2 minutes or until firm.

For Garnish: Boil lobster claws for 10-14 minutes. Cool and remove from shells. Cook leeks in butter over low heat until soft. Season with salt and pepper, add tomatoes, lobster claws and cook for 2 minutes more.

To serve, pour lobster beurre blanc into bowls, top with leek and tomato mixture and a cannelloni. Crown each with a lobster claw.

Marmalade Roasted Snapper with Sweet Potato Gnocchi

Serves four

4 snapper fillets, 6 oz each	3/4 cup orange marmalade
4 tblsps olive oil	3/4 cup fish stock (pg 99)
12 orange segments	6 oz whole butter
12 lime segments	4 tblsps diced tomatoes
24 sweet potato gnocchi	2 tblsps chiffonade chives
4 cups micro pea vines	salt & pepper to taste

Season the snapper with salt and pepper, then sear in olive oil on high heat on both sides. Set aside. Combine the fish stock and orange marmalade, bring to a boil and reduce by 1/3. Reduce the heat to low and whisk in 4 oz of butter. Remove from heat. Place the snapper in a 350°oven and finish cooking for about 4 to 6 minutes, depending on thickness of the fillets. Place the gnocchi in boiling salted water. When the gnocchi float to the top, remove and place them in the marmalade broth. Heat the broth on a simmer. Saute the pea vines and tomatoes in remaining butter and season with salt and pepper. Arrange the pea vines and snapper on plates, then garnish with gnocchi, chives, orange and lime segments.

Sweet Potato Gnocchi

3/4 lb peeled sweet potatoes	1/4 tsp nutmeg
3 qts water	1 tblsp truffle oil
2 tblsps chiffonade chives	salt & pepper to taste
2 tblsps brown sugar	1 cup flour

Boil sweet potatoes until tender, drain, refrigerate to cool. Push potatoes through food mill into a bowl, add chives, brown sugar, nutmeg, truffle oil and fold together. Add salt, pepper, half the flour and fold together. Add remaining flour until dough forms a ball. Separate 2-3 oz of dough at a time and on a floured surface roll into a rope shape 1/2" in diameter. Cut the gnocchi into 1" segments, pinch in the center and set aside to cook.

Chipolte Roasted Pork Tenderloin
Black Bean & Chorizo Stew

Serves four

1 pork tenderloin, 1 lb
1/2 cup chipolte tomato marinade (pg 98)
1 ear Todd's sweet corn
2 oz butter
1 cup milk
2 cups water

1/4 cup sugar
1/2 cup black bean stew
8 fried plantain slices
8 chives stems
salt & pepper to taste

Marinate the pork for 2-3 hours in chipolte marinade. Season with salt and pepper and grill until 140° internal temperature. Remove, let rest then slice 3/8" thick. Fry the plantain slices in oil until crispy. Remove and season. Combine butter, milk, water and sugar then bring to a boil. Blanch the corn for 8-10 minutes, remove and slice on the bias into four pieces. Warm the black bean stew and serve with pork, corn and plantain slices. Garnish with chives.

Black Bean Stew
1/4 lb ground chorizo
1/2 cup black beans, cooked
2 tblsps diced red pepper
2 tblsps diced red onion
2 tblsps chopped garlic
1/2 tsp cumin
1 tblsp sherry wine vinegar
salt & pepper to taste
2 tblsps olive oil
1 oz butter
2 tblsps chopped cilantro

Saute the onions, garlic and peppers in olive oil for 2-3 minutes. Add ground chorizo and cook until done. Lower heat and add sherry vinegar, black beans and cumin. Simmer for 5-6 minutes, stir in butter, cilantro and season with salt and pepper.

Foie Gras with Truffle Omelette & Shiitake Mushrooms

Serves four

1/2 lb foie gras
1 tblsp diced red pepper
1 tsp diced plum tomato
1 tblsp diced red onion
1/4 cup blanched asparagus tips
1 tblsp chopped chives
1 tblsp chopped basil
8 whole eggs
sliced truffles as garnish
2 tblsps butter
salt & pepper to taste
1 baguette

For the Omelette:
Beat the eggs, season with salt and pepper and set aside. Saute the onions, peppers and asparagus in butter in a 10" saute pan until tender. Add the tomatoes, chives, basil and stir in the eggs. Once the omelette is cooked, remove from pan and cut into four mini omelettes using a 3" cutter.

1 cup julienned shiitake mushrooms
2 tblsps sliced green onions
1 tblsp chiffonade basil
1 tblsp diced roasted tomato
2 tblsps butter
1/4 cup veal stock
salt & pepper to taste

For the Shiitake Mushrooms:
Lightly saute all the ingredients in butter until tender. Add veal stock and cook until thickened. Season with salt and pepper.

Season the foie gras with pepper and pan sear on medium heat for about 30 seconds on each side. Place the omelettes on top of the mushrooms, then top with the foie gras and garnish with truffle slices and toasted baguette slices.

70

My Surf & Turf with
Baby Spinach & Asiago Polenta

Serves four

4 tenderloin filets, 6 oz each
4 cold water lobster tails, 6 oz each
4 tblsps butter
1 lemon
8 cups fresh baby spinach

1 tblsp roasted garlic
2 tblsps sliced shallots
2 roasted red peppers (pg 99)
salt and pepper to taste
1/2 tsp chopped fresh thyme
oyster mushrooms for garnish

Grill the filets to your desired internal temperature. Split the tails in half, leaving them in shells. Melt half the butter and pour over the lobster. Squeeze the juice from the lemon over tails and season with salt and pepper. Cook at 375° for 8 to 10 minutes.

Saute the baby spinach in the remaining butter with the garlic and shallots. Season with salt and pepper.

Slice roasted peppers into 4 circles. Place 1/4 cup of polenta in each 3 inch ring mold, follow with a pepper circle, then the spinach. Unmold and top each ring with a filet, lobster tail and mushrooms sauteed in butter. Sprinkle with fresh thyme.

Asiago Polenta
1 cup polenta
3 cups chicken stock
3 tblsps grated asiago cheese
2 tblsps sliced chives

2 tblsps chopped basil
2 tblsps chopped thyme
2 tblsps butter
salt and pepper to taste

Bring the stock to a boil and stir in the polenta. Stir with a wooden spoon for 5 to 7 minutes, then add the cheese, spices and butter. Season with salt and pepper.

Duck Confit with Truffle Polenta

Serves four

4 duck legs
2 tsps sea salt
2 tblsps cracked black peppercorns
6 cups duck fat
10 sprigs of thyme

Season the legs with salt and pepper and refrigerate unwrapped overnight. Place the duck legs in a dutch oven with the duck fat, thyme sprigs and cover. Cook over low heat for 2 hours. The meat should be very tender, coming off the bone. Remove the legs from the fat and let cool at room temperature.

To finish the Confit:
duck meat from legs
1/2 cup red wine sauce (pg 102)
1 tsp chopped thyme
1 tblsp roasted garlic

2 tblsps diced roasted tomatoes
1 tsp chopped chives
1 tblsp butter
3 tblsps chiffonade of spinach

Skin and remove the meat from the legs by pulling off in strips. Combine the meat and red wine sauce and simmer over low heat for 10 to 15 minutes. Add all other ingredients except spinach and cook for another 5 to 8 minutes. Remove from heat and stir in the spinach until wilted.

For Duck Breast:
2 duck breasts
2 tblsps minced thyme
salt & pepper to taste
truffle polenta (pg105)

Saute the breasts, skin side down, over low heat until browned. Turn and sear other side. Cook in a 350° oven for 4–6 minutes or internal temperature of 120°. Remove and let rest for 8–10 minutes. Serve confit over truffle polenta and top with 3 slices of duck breast.

Duck Breast, Foie Gras Terrine & Red Grape Vinaigrette

Serves four
Duck Breast & Salad:
2 duck breasts
salt & pepper to taste
minced thyme
1 cup mache greens
4 bundles of raisins on the vine
1/2 cup red grape vinaigrette (pg 97)

Slowly cook the duck breasts on medium heat, skin side down, until the skin is golden brown. Drain off the fat, season with salt, pepper and thyme. Turn the breasts over and place in a 350° oven for 4 to 6 minutes. Let the duck breasts rest for 8 to 10 minutes before slicing.

Foie Gras Terrine:
2 lbs grade A foie gras lobes
1-1/2 tblsps kosher salt
1 tsp white pepper
1/4 cup brandy

Clean and devein foie gras lobes. Season with salt and pepper, add the brandy and chill overnight. Return to room temperature. Line a 4" x 8" terrine mold with plastic wrap, leaving 3" to 4" over the sides. Place one lobe in the terrine and press flat. Set second lobe on top and press to eliminate air. Cover with overlapping plastic and place lid on terrine. Cook in a water bath in a preheated 220° oven for 1 hour or internal temperature of 130°. Remove and place in ice bath for 20 minutes. Flip lid to fit inside terrine and press to remove excess fat. Place weight on lid and refrigerate for 24 hours. Slice duck breasts and top with raisin bundles. Slice foie gras terrine and arrange on plate. Serve with mache greens and drizzle with red grape vinaigrette.

Wood Grilled Filet,
Truffle Mashed Potatoes
& Candied Shallot

Serves four

4 filets, 8 oz each
4 candied shallots
8 white asparagus spears
4 baby carrots
4 potato gaufrettes

1 tblsp shaved black truffle
roasted tomato slices (pg 98)
1/2 tblsp butter
1/2 tblsp chopped basil
salt and pepper to taste

Grill the filets for 4 minutes on each side for medium rare, then season with salt and pepper. Saute asparagus and carrots in butter and basil. Serve filets with truffle mashed potatoes and sauted vegetables. Garnish each with a potato gaufrette, candied shallot, roasted tomato slices and shaved black truffle.

Truffle Mashed Potatoes
4 yukon gold potatoes
1-1/2 quarts chicken stock
2 tblsps creme fraiche
4 oz butter
1 tblsp minced black truffle
truffle oil to taste
salt and pepper to taste

Candied Shallots
4 shallots
2 tblsps olive oil
2 tblsps brown sugar
1/2 cup port wine
1/2 tsp chopped fresh thyme
salt and pepper to taste

For Truffle Mashed Potatoes: Boil the potatoes in chicken stock until tender. Drain and blend with the remaining ingredients. Season to taste.

For Candied Shallots: Saute shallots in oil until golden brown. Add sugar, wine, thyme, then oven roast at 350° until tender. Season with salt and pepper.

Grove Farms Colorado Lamb
with Mint Risotto

2 racks of lamb, frenched

12 scallions

4 baby golden beets, peeled

4 broccoli raab stalks

8 white asparagus, peeled

4 baby carrots, peeled

12 oz mint risotto (pg 104)

1 cup red wine sauce (pg 102)

salt & pepper to taste

1/4 cup olive oil

2 tblsps chopped shallots

2 oz whole butter

Bring 2 quarts of salted water to a boil. Blanch the vegetables in boiling water as follows: Beets 3 to 4 minutes, asparagus 1-1/2 to 2 minutes, carrots 2 minutes and broccoli 45 seconds. Shock each vegetable in an ice water bath, pat dry and set aside.

Season the lamb racks with salt and pepper. Sear in olive oil over high heat on all sides. Then place in a 300° oven for 12 to 15 minutes or until 120° internal temperature. Let rest 5-8 minutes before slicing.

Saute shallots in butter over medium heat. Toss in the asparagus, carrots and broccoli and season with salt and pepper. Place in oven to keep warm. Slice beets into circles and add to vegetables. To plate, start with risotto, then vegetables, lamb chop and loin and finish with red wine sauce.

Braised Short Ribs & Sea Scallops

Serves four

6 beef short ribs
flour
1 tblsp vegetable oil
1/2 cup chopped onion
1/2 cup diced tomato
6 thyme sprigs
4 rosemary sprigs
2 cups dry red wine
2 cups beef stock

Dust the ribs in flour and sear them lightly in oil over medium heat for 5 to 7 minutes. Remove and set aside. Remove half the fat from pan, add onions and cook for 2 minutes. Add the red wine and reduce by half. Add the tomato and beef stock and cook for 8 to 10 minutes more. Place the ribs in a braising pan, add the sauce, rosemary and thyme sprigs and bake in a 250° oven for two hours or until meat is fork tender and sauce is thickened.

4 sea scallops
4 baby carrots
8 white asparagus
4 baby bok-choy
salt & pepper to taste
2 tblsps butter
1 tblsp minced shallots
1 tsp minced chives
1 tblsp chopped basil
2 tblsps olive oil

Blanch all the vegetables in boiling salted water separately, then shock in an ice bath and set aside. Season scallops with salt and pepper and sear in olive oil over medium to high heat for 2 to 3 minutes on each side. Do not overcook. Remove some meat from the short ribs, arrange on the plate and top with a scallop. Heat the vegetables in butter and season with basil and chives, salt and pepper. Heat the fava beans in their broth, arrange on plates and top with a bone-in short rib.

1 cup fava beans, shelled
2 tblsps diced carrots
2 tblsps minced onion
1 tblsp chopped basil
sugar to taste
1 cup beef stock
salt & pepper

For Fava Bean Ragout: Lightly blanch the fava beans in salted boiling water for 2 to 3 minutes, then drain. Place all the ingredients in a pot and stew until beans are tender and sauce is thickened. Season with salt and pepper.

Vahlrona Chocolate & Mascarpone Mousse Tower

1 lb Vahlrona dark chocolate
1 qt heavy cream, whipped
1/2 cup warm water
6 tblsps simple syrup
4 gelatin sheets
6 oz mascarpone cheese

Melt the dark chocolate in a double boiler. Bloom the gelatin in warm water until smooth. Combine the simple syrup with the gelatin. Add this mixture to the Mascarpone cheese and whip on medium speed until smooth. Add the melted chocolate to the Mascarpone mixture and combine thoroughly. Fold the chocolate mixture into the whipped cream.

6 oz Vahlrona dark chocolate
4 pvc pipes, 3" high by 2" diameter
4 triangle shaped transfer sheets
4 acetate 3" strips

Line the pvc with the acetate strips and fill with the chocolate mousse to 3/4 full, making sure the top is flat. Refrigerate for 2 hours. Melt the dark chocolate. Using a pallet knife coat the triangle sheets evenly with a thin layer of chocolate. Remove the chocolate mousse from the pvc and peel off the acetate. Line up the triangle sheet with the bottom of the mousse and roll the sheet around the mousse, leaving one end slightly open. Refrigerate for 30 minutes.

1 cup whipped cinnamon cream
confectioners' sugar
3/4 cup raspberry puree
20 raspberries
4 mint leaf tops

Garnish the plate with raspberry puree. Carefully pull away the transfer sheet and place the mousse tower on the plate. Garnish with cinnamon whipped cream, raspberries and mint. Sprinkle with confectioners' sugar.

Raspberry Soufflé

Serves four

12 chilled egg whites
1-1/2 tsps cream of tartar
1-1/4 cups confectioners' sugar
1/2 cup raspberry puree

1/2 pint fresh raspberries
1/4 cup whole butter
2 tblsps granulated sugar

Using a kitchen aid, whip egg whites at high speed for 30 to 40 seconds. Stop mixing and add the cream of tartar and confectioners' sugar. Whip at medium speed until the whites have stiff peaks with good density, volume and shine. Place half of the whites into a stainless bowl and slowly fold in the raspberry puree. Then add the remaining whites and fold in until incorporated. Lightly butter the inside of 4 souffle dishes and dust with the granulated sugar. Place 8 to 10 raspberries in the bottom of each dish, then spoon in the souffle mixture to fill the dishes 2 to 3 inches above the rim tops. Tap the dishes on a hard surface to eliminate any air pockets. Bake at 350° for 14 to 18 minutes. The souffles should rise and be firm.

...udding & Espresso Ice Cream

Custard

1-1/2 cups half & half
4 oz Vahlrona chocolate bar
1/8 cup butter
2 whole eggs & 1 egg yolk
1/3 cup brown sugar
1 lb banana bread
8 Vahlrona chocolate coins

Combine the sugar and eggs in a bowl and whip until smooth. Bring the half and half to a boil. Place the chocolate and butter in a bowl and add in the hot half and half. Mix until smooth. Add the chocolate mixture to the egg mixture and fold in. Let cool and reserve. Cut the banana bread into small cubes and fold into the custard. Fill four 3 inch ring molds half way with this mixture. Place 2 chocolate coins in the center and fill to the top with the custard mixture. Bake at 350° for 12 minutes. Serve with espresso ice cream (pg 101) and garnish with raspberries and mint.

Plantains Foster & Funnel Cake

Plantains Foster

4 tblsps butter	2 ripe plantains, sliced
1 cup dark brown sugar	1/2 cup dark rum
1/4 cup banana liquor	1/4 cup orange juice
1 tblsp cinnamon	1/4 cup toasted macadamia nuts, chopped

In a skillet, heat the butter on low, add the brown sugar to make a paste. Add the plantain slices and cook until lightly browned and tender. Add the rum and banana liquor. Turn heat to high and flame off the rum. Add the cinnamon and simmer until thickened. Spoon the sauce over the funnel cake, top with macadamia nuts and your choice of ice cream.

Funnel Cake

3 eggs
2 cups milk
3-1/2 cups flour
1/3 cup sugar
pinch of salt
1 tblsp baking powder
confectioners' sugar
oil for deep frying

Beat the eggs with the milk. Sift together the flour, sugar, salt and baking powder, then add to the egg mixture. Beat until smooth. Heat the oil to 350°. Fill a pastry bag with a small tip 3/4 full with the batter. Let the batter stream into the oil in a circular pattern, making two cakes for each guest, one 4" and a smaller one for garnish. Top the cakes with powdered sugar.

Ice Cream & Sorbet Tasting

For the Raspberry Sorbet:
Heat one cup of water in a sauce pan, add the sugar and cook until sugar is dissolved. Bring to a boil, then simmer for 3 minutes and let cool. Puree the raspberries with the other cup of water and strain through a sieve. Stir the raspberry and syrup mixtures together. Taste and add more sugar if desired. Freeze mixture in an ice cream machine. Store in your freezer.

4 cups raspberries
juice from 1 lemon
2 cups water
1 cup sugar

3 cups heavy cream
1 cup milk
8 egg yolks
3/4 cup sugar

1 vanilla bean
8 oz creamy peanut butter
8 oz chocolate coins

For Ice Cream Base: Combine cream and milk in a sauce pan. Split vanilla bean, scrape out seeds and add both pod and seeds to milk mixture. Bring mixture to a simmer and cook for 10 minutes. Combine sugar and egg yolks and whip until pale and fluffy. Slowly add about 1/2 of the hot cream to the egg mixture. Then pour this mixture back into the remaining hot cream. Return to heat and cook to 165° stirring constantly. Strain through a sieve and cool mixture for 3-4 hours. Add mixture to an ice cream machine and follow directions for freezing.

For Peanut Butter Swirl: Warm peanut butter until soft. Remove ice cream base from machine and fold in peanut butter. Place in freezer overnight.

For Chocolate Ice Cream: Replace vanilla bean with chocolate and follow recipe above.

& Sea Scallops

Vegetable

...our and sear them lightly in oil
...for 5 to 7 minutes. Remove
...ve half the fat from pan.
...r 2 minutes. Add the
...half. Add the tomato
...8 to 10 minutes
...ising pan, add the
...rigs and bal...

Vinaigrettes

Citrus Vinaigrette

1/2 cup chopped shallots
3/4 cup fresh orange juice
1/4 cup brown sugar
1/4 cup rice wine vinegar

1/2 cup grapeseed oil
1 tsp minced chives
1 tsp chopped tarragon
salt & pepper to taste.

In a blender, combine shallots, orange juice, sugar, vinegar, chives and tarragon and puree until smooth. Slowly add the grapeseed oil and blend until completely emulsified. Season with salt and pepper.

Truffle Vinaigrette

1/2 cup plus 2 tblsps grapeseed oil
2 tblsps champagne vinegar
1 tblsp sherry wine vinegar
1 tblsp chopped shallots
1 tblsp dijon mustard

1 tblsp chopped truffles
1 tsp white truffle oil
1 tblsp chopped roasted garlic
1 tsp fresh lemon juice
salt & pepper to taste

In a blender, combine the vinegars, shallots, mustard, truffles and garlic until smooth. On medium speed, slowly add grapeseed oil and blend until completely emulsified. Pour into a bowl, add lemon juice and truffle oil, then season with salt and pepper.

Soy Vinaigrette

3/4 cup soy sauce

1/3 cup rice wine vinegar

2 tblsps fresh orange juice

1 tsp sirachi (Thai chili sauce)

1-1/2 tblsp chopped garlic

1 tblsp brown sugar

2 tblsps chopped green onion

1 tblsp chopped fresh cilantro

2 tblsps sesame oil

Combine all ingredients in a blender and puree until smooth.

Petite Syrah Vinaigrette

1-1/4 cups Petite Syrah wine

1 cup olive oil

1/4 cup champagne vinegar

2 tsps roasted garlic puree

3 tsps chopped shallots

1 tsp chopped rosemary

1 tsp chopped thyme

1 tsp chopped basil

3 tsps honey

1/4 cup water

salt & pepper to taste

Combine all ingredients in a blender and puree until completely emulsified.

Red Grape Vinaigrette

1 cup sliced red seedless grapes

1 tsp minced shallots

1/2 cup champagne vinegar

1/4 cup olive oil

1/4 cup red wine

1 tsp sugar

1/4 cup picked chervil

fresh ground pepper

Combine ingredients in a bowl then whisk in the olive oil. Season with salt if needed.

Tomato Chipotle Marinade

2 tblsps chopped garlic
2 chipolte peppers, chopped
4 oz sundried tomatoes
2 tblsps julienned red onion
2 tblsps julienned red pepper
2 tblsps chicken stock

1/2 tsp cumin
1 tblsp chopped cilantro
1 tblsp brown sugar
2 tblsps olive oil

Saute garlic, onions and peppers over high heat 2-3 minutes. Reduce heat to low and add tomatoes, chipotle peppers, and chicken stock. Cover and simmer 15-20 minutes. Remove from heat and stir in cumin, cilantro and brown sugar. Cool to room temperature. In a food processor on medium speed, add oil very slowly to mixture until fully incorporated. Remove and refrigerate.

Tomato Confit

16 red pear tomatoes, halved
16 yellow pear tomatoes, halved
2 shallots, julienned
2 garlic cloves, finely sliced
1/4 cup sugar

1-1/2 tblsps orange zest
juice of 1 orange
1/3 cup extra virgin olive oil
2 tblsps chiffonade basil
salt and pepper to taste

Toss together the first seven ingredients. Add the oil and bake in an oven proof dish at 200° for 15 to 20 minutes. Remove from the oven, add basil, then season with salt and pepper. Serve warm over a bed of spinach.

Roasted Tomatoes

2 plum tomatoes, sliced thin
4 tblsps olive oil
1 tblsp picked thyme leaves

1 tblsp sugar
salt and pepper to taste

Place tomato slices on a cookie sheet and sprinkle with olive oil, thyme, sugar, salt and pepper. Bake in a 250° oven for 30 to 45 minutes or until just dry. Let cool.

Red Pepper Juice

4 red peppers
1 shallot
1/2 garlic clove, sliced

1 thyme sprig
salt & pepper to taste

Halve the peppers, remove stems and seeds, then process through a vegetable juicer. Combine juice with shallot, garlic, thyme and cook over medium heat. Reduce to a syrup consistency. Season with salt and pepper, strain and cool.

Vanilla Bean Mashed Potatoes

1-1/2 lbs yukon gold potatoes
1/4 cup sour cream
5 oz whole butter

2 tblsps vanilla extract
1 vanilla bean
salt & pepper to taste

Cook potatoes in boiling water until tender. Drain and let rest for 1 minute. Combine the sour cream, butter, vanilla extract and the seeds scraped from the vanilla bean. Using a food mill, whisk the potatoes into the sour cream and butter mixture. Season with salt and pepper.

Roasted Peppers

2 red peppers
2 tblsps olive oil
kosher salt as needed

Coat the peppers with the oil, by hand, to ensure peppers are completely coated. Season with salt and roast at 375° until skin color begins to blacken. Place in a bowl and cover for 20 minutes. Remove the skin and seeds from peppers.

Fish Stock

5 lbs fish bones (from white fish)
1-1/2 cups chopped celery
1-1/2 cups chopped onion
1 cup whole basil leaves
1 tblsp white peppercorns

2 bay leaves
2 tomatoes, sliced thin

Rinse fish bones under cold water until water runs clear. In the bottom of a heavy stock pot layer celery, onion, basil, peppercorns and bay leaves. Add fish bones and fill the pot with enough water to cover the bones. Top with the tomato halves, cook over low heat and bring to a simmer. Simmer another 20 to 30 minutes then strain carefully, keeping the stock as clear as possible.

Papaya Banana Chutney

2 papayas, finely diced
2 bananas, finely diced
1 cup orange juice
1/2 cup brown sugar
1 tblsp chopped fresh ginger
2 tblsps chiffonade mint

Combine orange juice, sugar, ginger and reduce over medium high heat by half. Add the papaya and bananas and cook for an additional 8 to 10 minutes on medium to low heat. Cool then add the mint.

Papaya Banana Ravioli

4 cups all purpose flour
5 extra large eggs
1 tblsp olive oil
1 tblsp salt

Using a fork, create a well in the flour and place eggs, oil and salt in the center. Slowly incorporate flour until dough forms a ball. Continue until all flour is incorporated, then refrigerate. Starting with the #1 setting, roll pasta dough through a pasta machine several times, ending with the #5 setting. Place 1 tablespoon of Papaya Banana Chutney every 2 to 2-1/2 inches in center of pasta sheet. Fold pasta dough over and seal each ravioli by pressing your fingers around the chutney. Use a round cutter to cut out raviolis. Place in boiling water and cook for 3 minutes. Drain well.

Espresso Ice Cream

2 cups half and half
3/4 cup sugar
8 egg yolks
2 espresso pods

Open the espresso pods, add to the half and half and heat to a simmer for 20 minutes. Strain through a cheese cloth. In a separate bowl, combine the eggs and sugar and whip until smooth. Temper this mixture with a little of the hot half and half then combine with remaining half and half. Return to low heat and cook to 160°, stirring constantly. Strain and shock in ice bath. Once cooled, make ice cream using an ice cream machine.

Wasabi Mayonnaise

3 egg yolks
1-1/2 cups vegetable oil
1 tsp white vinegar
1/2 tsp wasabi powder
1/2 tsp mustard powder
3 tsps lemon juice
1 tsp sugar
salt and white pepper to taste

Combine egg yolks, sugar, mustard and wasabi powders and whip until thick and fluffy. Add 1/4 of the oil slowly while whipping at medium speed. Mix the vinegar and lemon juice then add to egg mixture. Season with salt and pepper and refrigerate.

Sauces & Glazes

Red Wine Sauce

2 tblsps olive oil
3 tblsps chopped shallot   1/2 tsp peppercorns
1/4 cup chopped onion   4 to 6 sprigs of thyme
1/4 cup chopped celery   1-1/2 cups demi glace
1/4 cup chopped carrot   1-1/2 oz butter
1 cup Cabernet or Merlot   salt and pepper to taste

Heat the oil in a pan and saute the shallot, onion, celery and carrot until caramelized. Deglaze the pan with red wine and reduce by 2/3. Add the peppercorns, thyme and demi glace, then simmer until reduced by 1/3. Remove from heat and strain. Season, add butter and stir until completely combined.

Demi Glace

8 lbs veal marrow bones (shanks)
1/2 cup olive oil   1 cup tomato paste
2 cups chopped celery   8 to 10 sprigs of thyme
2 cups chopped onion   2 tblsps peppercorns
2 cups chopped carrot   3 bay leaves
3 tomatoes, quartered   1-1/2 to 2 gals cold water

Have bones cut into pieces. Coat bones with 1/4 cup olive oil. Place in a heavy roasting pan and cook at 350° until they begin to brown. Toss the celery, onion and carrot in the remaining 1/4 cup oil and add to roasting pan. Cook until vegetables have caramelized. Place bones and vegetables in a stock pot, add remaining ingredients and water. Bring stock to a simmer and cook for 6 to 8 hours, removing grease as needed. Strain, return to heat and reduce by 2/3. Strain and refrigerate.

Lobster Beurre Blanc (Coral Butter)

1 lb lobster heads
1 cup chopped celery
1 cup chopped onion
1 cup chopped tomato
1 tblsp tomato paste
1 cup white wine
1/4 cup brandy

1 qt heavy cream
8 oz whole butter, cubed
1/4 cup clarified butter
1 tblsp peppercorns
1 tblsp chopped thyme
1 tblsp chopped basil
salt and pepper to taste

Remove organs from lobster heads and rinse thoroughly. Chop into small pieces and saute in clarified butter over medium heat 2 to 3 minutes. Add the vegetables and peppercorns and cook for 1 to 2 minutes more. Deglaze pan with the brandy. Add the white wine and cook until liquid is almost gone. Add the heavy cream, tomato paste and reduce heat. Simmer for 15 to 20 minutes, reducing by 1/3. Remove from heat, add herbs and let sit for 2 to 3 minutes. Slowly stir in the whole butter then strain. Season with salt and pepper.

Vanilla Beurre Blanc

2 shallots, chopped
1 tsp white peppercorns
1 tsp black peppercorns
1 tblsps chopped cilantro
1 vanilla bean, split

1/4 cup white wine
1/4 cup clarified butter
1 cup heavy cream
1 lb cold butter, sliced

Combine the first 7 ingredients in a sauce pot and cook over low heat for 10 minutes until shallots are opaque. Add the cream, increase the heat to medium and cook until reduced by 3/4 and thickened. Remove from heat. Add butter, mix well then strain.

Sweet Asian Glaze

1 cup sweetened chili sauce
1/2 cup light soy sauce
1/4 cup honey
1/4 cup sweet soy sauce

1/4 cup rice wine vinegar
1 tblsp julienned pickled ginger
1 tblsp fresh chopped cilantro

Combine all ingredients and mix well. Chill for at least 1 hour.

Grains

Saffron Risotto

5 tblsps olive oil

6 cups fish stock

1 medium onion, minced

2-1/2 cups arborio rice

pinch of saffron threads

3/4 cup white wine

1/2 cup asiago cheese

1/4 cup whole butter

Heat the olive oil and cook the onions until tender. Add the rice and saffron, stirring to coat the rice well. Add the wine and cook until evaporated, stirring continuously. Continue stirring and add the fish stock 1/4 cup at a time until the stock is absorbed. Repeat this process until the rice is tender. Remove from heat and fold in the butter and cheese, then season with salt and pepper.

Mint Risotto

5 tblsps extra virgin olive oil

6 cups chicken stock

1 cup diced onion

2-1/2 cups arborio rice

3/4 cup white wine

2 oz butter

1/2 cup mint pesto

salt and pepper to taste

Mint Pesto

2 tblsps mint leaves

2 tblsps parsley leaves

1 tblsp chopped roasted garlic

1/4 cup toasted pine nuts

1/2 cup extra virgin olive oil

2 tblsps grated asiago cheese

For the Risotto: Saute the onion in oil over medium high heat until soft. Add the rice and saute for 2 minutes more. Add the wine, stir and cook until evaporated. Add about 1/2 cup stock and cook, stirring constantly, until absorbed. Continue adding stock this way until rice is cooked. Remove from heat and stir in butter and pesto then season.

For the Pesto: Place mint and parsley leaves in a blender with the garlic and pine nuts. Add the oil and blend at high speed until finely pureed. Pour into a bowl and fold in the cheese.

Coconut Jasmine Rice

2 tblsps chopped ginger
1-1/2 tblsps chopped garlic
1 can coconut milk (14 oz)
1-3/4 cups chicken stock

3 tblsps chopped cilantro
1/2 cup sugar
1-3/4 cups jasmine rice
1-1/2 tblsps sesame oil
salt and pepper to taste

Heat oil over medium heat and saute the garlic and ginger for 1 minute. Deglaze pan with chicken stock then add the coconut milk and bring to a boil. Stir in rice, reduce heat and cover. Cook for 20 to 25 minutes, stirring occasionally, until liquid is absorbed. Remove from heat and add cilantro and sugar. Mix well and season with salt and pepper.

Sushi Rice

2 cups sushi rice (short grain)
2 cups water
2-1/2 tblsps rice wine vinegar

3/4 tblsp salt
1 tsp Mirin
2-1/2 tblsps sugar

Rinse the rice several times in cool water. Let rice rest 15 to 20 minutes before cooking. Place in a rice cooker and cook according to instructions. When finished, turn the cooker off and leave rice covered an additional 10 minutes to steam. Meanwhile, combine the vinegar, sugar, salt, Mirin and warm. Remove rice from cooker and thoroughly coat with vinegar mixture. Spread on a platter, cover with a damp cloth and cool to room temperature.

Truffle Polenta

1/2 cup polenta
2 cups chicken stock
3 tblsps diced red onion
2 tblsps diced black truffles

1 tblsp chopped thyme
1 tsp chopped chives
3 tblsps asiago cheese
2 tblsps butter
salt and pepper to taste

Bring the chicken stock and onions to a boil. Lower the heat and slowly stir in the polenta. Continue to stir for approximately 5 minutes until the polenta is soft and smooth. Remove from heat and stir in the truffles, thyme, chives and cheese. Add the butter and season with salt and pepper.

Culinary Clues

Agnolotti: Italian for "priests' caps", describing small, crescent-shaped stuffed pasta.

Ahi tuna: the Hawaiian name for yellowfin, as well as bigeye tuna.

Bonito flakes: made from bonito tuna, dried and used in many Japanese dishes.

Chiffonade: a french phrase meaning "made of rags". Culinarily, it refers to thin strips or shreds of vegetables.

Cipollini: these bittersweet bulbs of the grape hyacinth taste and look like small onions. Can be found in Italian markets during the fall.

Confit: derived from an ancient method of preserving meat whereby it is salted and slowly cooked in its own fat.

Creme fraiche: a matured, thickened cream with a slightly tangy, nutty flavor and velvety rich texture.

Crostini: meaning "little toasts" in Italian, are small thin slices of toasted bread usually brushed with olive oil.

Frenched: to trim meat away from the end of a rib. Also to cut vegetables or meat into very thin strips lengthwise.

Frisée: a member of the chicory family with delicate slender, curly leaves and a mildly bitter flavor. Often used in special salad mixes.

Galette: a round, rather flat cake or tart made with meat, cheese, fruit or many other ingredients.

Gaufrette: potato gaufrettes are thin, latticed, fan-shaped wafers used as garnish on meat dishes.

Persicus caviar: a high quality Iranian caviar.

Polenta: a staple of northern Italy, polenta is a mush made from cornmeal. It can be eaten hot with a little butter or cooled until firmed, cut into squares and fried.

Quenelle: a light delicate dumpling made of seasoned, minced or ground fish, meat or vegetables.

Salsify: a root vegetable also known as oyster plant because of its taste. Found in Spanish, Italian or Greek markets.

Semolina: durum wheat that is more coarsely ground than normal flours. Most good pastas are made from semolina.

JNDEX

DON CeSAR BEACH RESORT

A LOEWS HOTEL

ST PETE BEACH

First Published in the USA by Espichel Enterprises

Managing Editor: Susan Eanes
Culinary Food Stylist & Recipes: Eric Neri, Executive Chef
Book Design & Photography: Charles Eanes
Photography: Tobby Rau

Library of Congress Control Number: 2004097136
ISBN   1-890494-08-9
Printed in the USA

DON CESAR BEACH RESORT, A LOEWS HOTEL
3400 GULF BOULEVARD
ST. PETE BEACH
FLORIDA 33706

PHONE 727 360 1881 ~ 800 282 1116
www.doncesar.com   www.loewshotels.com